Keep this pocket-sized
you are visiting Southar

Whether you are in   ., you will
enjoy an evocative journey back in time. Compare
the Southampton of old with what you can see
today—see how the streets of the city and its
surrounding towns and villages have changed, how
shops and buildings have been altered or replaced;
look at fine details such as lamp-posts, shop fascias
and trade signs. See the many alterations to the
Southampton region that have taken place
during our lives, and which we may have taken for
granted.

At the turn of a page you will gain fascinating
insights into Southampton's unique history.

FRANCIS FRITH'S
pocket ALBUM

SOUTHAMPTON AND DISTRICT

A POCKET ALBUM

Adapted from an original book by
NICK CHANNER

First published in the United Kingdom in 2003 by
Frith Book Company Ltd
Reprinted 2004

ISBN 1-85937-714-9

British Library Cataloguing in Publication Data

Southampton and District—A Pocket Album
Adapted from an original book by Nick Channer

Frith Book Company Ltd
Frith's Barn, Teffont,
Salisbury, Wiltshire SP3 5QP
Tel: +44 (0) 1722 716 376
Email: info@francisfrith.co.uk
www.francisfrith.co.uk

Printed and bound in Great Britain by MPG, Bodmin

Front Cover: Above Bar 1900 / S151001
The colour-tinting is for illustrative purposes only, and is not intended to be historically accurate.

Frontispiece: Southampton, High Street 1908 / 60420

CONTENTS

FRANCIS FRITH
VICTORIAN PIONEER

Francis Frith, founder of the world-famous photographic archive, was a complex and multi-talented man. A devout Quaker and a highly successful Victorian businessman, he was philosophical by nature and pioneering in outlook. By 1855 he had already established a wholesale grocery business in Liverpool, and sold it for the astonishing sum of £200,000, which is the equivalent today of over £15,000,000. Now in his thirties, and captivated by the new science of photography, Frith set out on a series of pioneering journeys up the Nile and to the Near East.

INTRIGUE AND EXPLORATION

He was the first photographer to venture beyond the sixth cataract of the Nile. Africa was still the mysterious 'Dark Continent', and Stanley and Livingstone's historic meeting was a decade into the future. The conditions for picture taking confound belief. He laboured for hours in his wicker dark-room in the sweltering heat of the desert, while the volatile chemicals fizzed dangerously in their trays. Back in London he exhibited his photographs and was 'rapturously cheered' by members of the Royal Society. His reputation as a photographer was made overnight.

VENTURE OF A LIFE-TIME

By the 1870s the railways had threaded their way across the country, and Bank Holidays and half-day Saturdays had been made obligatory by Act of Parliament. All of a sudden the working man and his family were able to enjoy days out, take holidays, and see a little more of the world.

With typical business acumen, Francis Frith foresaw that these new tourists would enjoy having souvenirs to commemorate their days out. For the next thirty years he travelled the country by train and by pony and trap, producing fine photographs of seaside resorts and beauty spots that were keenly bought by millions of Victorians. These prints were painstakingly pasted into family albums and pored over during the dark nights of winter, rekindling precious memories of summer excursions. Frith's studio was soon supplying retail shops all over the country, and by 1890 F Frith & Co had become the greatest specialist photographic publishing company in the world, with over 2,000 sales outlets, and pioneered the picture postcard.

FRANCIS FRITH'S LEGACY

Francis Frith had died in 1898 at his villa in Cannes, his great project still growing. The archive he created continued in business for another seventy years. By 1970 it contained over a third of a million pictures showing 7,000 British towns and villages.

Frith's legacy to us today is of immense significance and value, for the magnificent archive of evocative photographs he created provides a unique record of change in the cities, towns and villages throughout Britain over a century and more. Frith and his fellow studio photographers revisited locations many times down the years to update their views, compiling for us an enthralling and colourful pageant of British life and character.

We are fortunate that Frith was dedicated to recording the minutiae of everyday life. For it is this sheer wealth of visual data, the painstaking chronicle of changes in dress, transport, street layouts, buildings, housing, engineering and landscape that captivates us so much today, offering us a powerful link with the past and with the lives of our ancestors.

Computers have now made it possible for Frith's many thousands of images to be accessed almost instantly. The archive offers every one of us an opportunity to examine the places where we and our families have lived and worked down the years. Its images, depicting our shared past, are now bringing pleasure and enlightenment to millions around the world a century and more after his death.

FLOATING BRIDGE c1955 / W468003

SOUTHAMPTON
AN INTRODUCTION

SOUTHAMPTON and Hampshire's strongly defended coastline are an intrinsic part of Britain's history. Acting as a symbolic gateway to the world, Southampton Water is the wide estuary of two great rivers —the Test and the Itchen. In the golden days of ocean-going travel, this internationally famous waterway provided first-time visitors to these shores with one of the first glimpses of English soil. Today, the waterfront is more heavily industrialised and the great passenger liners are certainly fewer. But the sense of maritime history is still tangible as one recalls the names of the great liners which once plied these historic waters - the 'Mauretania', the 'Aquitania', the 'Queen Mary' and the 'Queen Elizabeth' among them. The 'Titanic' sailed from Southampton in 1912, and the 'Great Eastern' was moored in Southampton Water prior to her maiden voyage in 1861.

Southampton Water has also played a key role in the development of flying boats and sea-planes, which is superbly illustrated in the city's Hall of Aviation. Today, the scene is still a bustling one: you do not have to wait long before you spot an oil tanker, a tug or a ferry, and the low roar of the hydrofoil may arouse your interest as it zips in and out of Southampton Docks. There is always something worth seeing on Southampton Water. But what of the city?

Think of Southampton and we tend to think of passenger liners, freight traffic and ferries. For 500 years it was one of England's leading ports, synonymous with shipbuilding and cruise liners. However, take a stroll through Southampton today and you will see that it is a fascinating mix of ancient and modern. This is a city that has much more to offer than its sprawling docks and bustling waterfront.

An obvious stop on any tour of Southampton has to be the Hall of Aviation. This entertaining attraction is a fitting memorial to the achievements of R J Mitchell, who designed the famous Spitfire fighter aircraft. Here, visitors can climb up to the flight deck of the legendary Sandringham flying boat around which the hall was built. The inside of the flying boat is reminiscent of a first class railway carriage, a classic reminder of the great days of luxury travel. Southampton Water was where these wonderful flying machines used to take off and land; it was a centre for early experimental flying and later a base for long-distance flights.

Not far from the Hall of Aviation is a stark reminder of the 'Titanic'. The old Terminus station, which was opened in 1840 and is still regarded as a wonderful example of classic railway architecture, is where passengers bound for the doomed ship arrived, spending the night at the majestic South Western Hotel prior to her departure the following day. A small quayside memorial marks the spot where the 'Titanic' was berthed prior to her ill-fated maiden voyage in April 1912.

Further along the quay we can begin to trace the old town wall, which dates back to about 1350. This is the start of a walk into history, taking us round the medieval town of Hampton, as Southampton used to be known, and visiting many interesting buildings and landmarks en route. Begin by having a look at the 15th-century God's House Tower, originally the south-east gate of the old town and one of the earliest artillery fortifications in Europe. Heading north brings us to the ruined church of Holy Rood, erected in 1320 and damaged by enemy bombing on the night of 13 November 1940. Known for centuries as the 'church of the sailors', its ruins have been preserved by the people of the city as a memorial and garden of rest dedicated to those who served in the Merchant Navy and lost their lives at sea. There is also a memorial to the stewards, sailors and firemen who perished in the 'Titanic' disaster.

Our next objective is Bargate, one of the finest medieval gateways in the country, dating back to the late 12th century. A pleasant stroll through the city parks brings us to the statue of Richard Andrews, a 19th-century coach-builder who was five times mayor of Southampton. The statue was unveiled in 1860, a year after his death. This corner of the city is littered with grand monuments. The 'Titanic' memorial recalls the engineer-officers who 'showed their high conception of duty and heroism by remaining at their posts', and nearby is Southampton's awesome cenotaph, designed by Edwin Lutyens. Close by is an imposing monument to Issac Watts, the famous hymn-writer, who was a native of the city.

Heading south again, back towards the quay, brings us to Portland Terrace, its elegant Regency design and wrought-iron balconies recalling Southampton's days as a fashionable spa town and resort. Our tour concludes with a return to the old town walls. Soon we reach Arundel Tower and Catchcold Tower, upon which there was an anti-aircraft gun during the Second World War. Shortly we reach the remains of the old castle and the site of the earliest fortifications for the ancient port. Evidence suggests that there may have been a quay here, in the days when seawater reached this far inland. Castle Water Gate, as it is known, may well have had wooden, detachable steps running down to the water's edge.

Beyond Castle Water Gate, we come to Pilgrims Gate, where we leave the old wall and make for the Tudor House overlooking St Michael's Square. This striking timber-framed building dates back to about 1500 and includes some fascinating photographs of Southampton in previous years. Make time to have a look at the Tudor garden which occupies a delightful hidden corner of the city.

From here our route takes us south along Bugle Street to Westgate. Henry V marched his army through here on its way to Agincourt. Adjacent to Westgate is the Tudor Merchant Hall, which was moved from St Michael's Square to its present site in 1634. From here we make for the waterfront and the Wool House, now a maritime museum, which explains in fascinating detail Southampton's role as one of the world's great ports. Nearby is the Mayflower memorial, which commemorates the sailing of the Pilgrim Fathers in 1620, and across the road is the crumbling Royal Pier, damaged by fire in the 1980s.

Francis Frith's photographs of Southampton offer a fascinating glimpse into the changing face of a city. Changes in fashion, shopping and public transport are all represented here, with Frith's images serving as a permanent record of the times. Outside Southampton his photographs of villages and country towns also serve as a reminder of how life used to be. Many of these communities have expanded and evolved almost beyond recognition over the years, while others have stayed largely the same, retaining their distinctive character and identity. The centre of Botley, for example, looks much the same today as it did in the 1950s and '60s when Frith first photographed it. Bursledon and Hamble, on the shores of Southampton Water, are equally timeless in their look and appeal.

Use this book to compare a way of life that many of us still fondly remember with the reality of the present day, examining the numerous changes in urban and rural life, the cars, the buildings, the way we looked and the way we were. These fascinating pictures tell us more about ourselves than we might think. Our memories serve us well, but time and distance lend a certain enchantment that can distort the truth. Francis Frith's photographs, offering a unique social record of the past, can never lie.

Many of the buildings in Southampton's famous High Street were destroyed during the Second World War, more than 30 years after this Frith photograph was taken. Horse-drawn trams were introduced to the city in 1879 and electrified in 1900. The tram on the right carries an advert for Brasso. On the left is a large sign for Liptons, the well-known family grocer.

HIGH STREET

1908 / 60418

HIGH STREET

1908 / 60420

Note the tram lines running down the middle of the street. On the left is the imposing Georgian church of All Saints, built in 1795. Badly damaged during World War Two, it was finally demolished in the 1950s. Jane Austen knew this church and its minister, the Reverend Richard Mant. Ahead is the spire of St Lawrence's Church, which was pulled down in 1929 after it became redundant.

ABOVE BAR

1900 / S151001

This picture shows Bargate facing south. There were once seven gates into Southampton's old walled town. Walk the walls today and only five can be seen. Signs for Seville Orange Marmalade and Strongs Romsey Ales can be seen to the right of Bargate.

Up until the 1930s, specially designed trams with dome-shaped tops to fit the arch travelled through Bargate. The adjoining walls and buildings were subsequently destroyed so that traffic bypassed the gate. Rounded flanking towers can be seen in the photograph, and two lions stand either side of the pointed arch.

BARGATE

1908 / 60426

BARGATE

1908 / 60427

BARGATE

1908 / 60428

This early 20th-century photograph shows Bargate at its best. Characterised by pointed arches and fine stonework, the old gate is also renowned for its statue of George III gazing down the High Street, dressed as a Roman and wearing a toga.

Bargate was originally built to guard the main road into Southampton. Over the years it has been a toll-gate, prison, guildhall and museum. The original Norman arch dates back to about 1175, and the tower was added a century later. The upper floor used to be the guildhall. By the time this photograph was taken, the buildings either side of Bargate had been demolished to allow traffic to pass freely round each side of it.

BARGATE

c1955 / S151013

BARGATE

c1955 / S151009

OLD
TOWN
WALLS

1892 / 31335

Southampton's walls and defences were built from stone brought across from the Isle of Wight. This must have been a huge operation, considering that there were one and a quarter miles of walls, seven gates and 29 towers. Following the Norman invasion of 1066, Southampton became a key port, and the walls and other buildings are a permanent reminder of Southampton's wealth and prosperity in those days.

OLD TOWN WALLS

1892 / 31336

Westgate, dating back to the 14th century, provides access to the south-west corner of the old walled town. One of the finest and best preserved of these remaining fortifications, this was once the main gate to West Quay, which for many centuries was the only quay that could accommodate larger vessels, in the days when seawater reached this far inland. Westgate offers some idea of what it would have been like to live beside the city walls. The portcullis was removed in 1744 when it became 'a nuisance, and of no manner of use'.

WESTGATE

1908 / 60431

WESTGATE

1908 / 60430

The timber-framed Tudor House, one of the city's finest buildings, dates back to about 1500, and has hardly changed at all since this photograph was taken. It became a museum in 1911; many years later, in the early 1980s, its garden was opened to the public as a Tudor garden. Upstairs are aerial photographs of Southampton over the years.

TUDOR HOUSE

1908 / 60435

This famous monument commemorates the departure of the Pilgrim Fathers to America in August 1620. Travelling aboard the 'Mayflower', the emigrants had to put into Dartmouth and Plymouth following problems with the ship. The memorial was erected opposite the pier on Town Quay in 1913, 11 years before this photograph was taken.

PILGRIM FATHERS' MONUMENT

1924 / 76264

The Pilgrim Fathers' Monument is built of Portland stone and rises 50 feet above the ground. Just visible at the top is a beacon surrounded by Greek pillars and crowned by a copper model of the 'Mayflower' in the form of a weathervane. The ship set sail from nearby West Quay.

PILGRIM FATHERS' MONUMENT

1924 / 76265

On the right of the photograph is the 15th-century God's House Tower, formerly the south-east gate of the old town and one of the earliest artillery fortifications in Europe. A ditch ran alongside the building until the 1850s, which was intended to link Southampton with the Andover Canal and the River Test. This used to be the home of the town gunner, with the guns and powder stored here. During the 17th century, when it was the town jail, prisoners of war were held in custody here.

THE OLD PRISON AND SOUTH GATE

1908 / 60429

ROYAL PIER PAVILION

1908 / 60415

The Royal Pier, at the eastern end of Mayflower Park, was opened in 1833 and for many years was the largest in the south of England. The pier was reconstructed during the early 1890s, and the pavilion's distinctive onion domes were added in the late 1920s. Much of it was destroyed by fire in 1987.

Here we see the 'Finland' in Number 6 Dry Dock. The vessel was not a regular visitor to the port, and could have been here on charter. Southampton's other main dry dock, Trafalgar, was opened in 1905 and probably would have been used by the 'Titanic' had she survived.

IN DRY DOCK

1908 / 60442

The name 'La Plata' was adopted by several ships from 1860 onwards. These vessels sailed to the West Indian islands and South America, carrying passengers and cargo.

THE DOCKS

1917 / S151002

At the heart of Southampton lies the Civic Centre, with its council offices, law courts and art gallery. The building dates back to the 1930s; soaring above it is the distinctive 182-ft high tower, visible from many parts of the city. Today, Southampton has one of the finest 20th-century British art collections outside London.

THE CIVIC CENTRE

c1955 / S151046

THE ANDREWS MONUMENT

The Common dates back to medieval times. It was purchased by the town from the manor of Shirley in 1228 for ten silver marks—quite a bargain! Today, no other city in England has such a large area of public common, and within its boundaries more than 350 species of flowering plants and over 100 species of birds have been identified. The rambling building at the centre of the photograph is The Cowheards pub.

ON THE COMMON

1908 / 60447

THE STAG GATES

1908 / 60443

A rather complex road junction now marks the spot where these gates once stood. The gates, signifying the entrance to the Bevois Mount Estate, date back to 1844, but were removed before World War Two. What eventually became of them is one of the city's enduring mysteries, though the stonework may have been used in the building of the parks rockery by Brunswick Place.

THE FLOATING BRIDGE

1908 / 60438

Southampton's famous Floating Bridge enabled foot passengers and traffic to cross the Itchen between the city and the south-eastern suburb of Woolston. The steam-powered floating bridge was in service for 141 years, between 1836 and 1977. A high-level road bridge eventually replaced it.

A fascinating picture of a suburban street. On the extreme left is Palmers, with John Bull tyres and cycle lamp batteries on display in the window. A few doors up is the distinctive façade of a small cinema, or 'flea pit' as they were sometimes known. Until comparatively recently every town had at least one cinema, and cities the size of Southampton often had scores of them. On the right is another relic of the old high street—the National Provincial Bank.

WOOLSTON

PORTSMOUTH ROAD c1960 / W468029

Founded in 1239 by the monks of Beaulieu Abbey, Netley Abbey occupies a pretty setting amidst the trees. Close by is Southampton Water. The abbey was dissolved in 1536 and later became a private mansion. In the 18th century it passed to a Southampton builder who was killed by falling tracery as he began to demolish the site.

NETLEY

THE ABBEY 1908 / 60468

NETLEY

THE ABBEY CLOISTERS 1908 / 60471

The church of St Edward the Confessor contains a medieval effigy of a crusader monk, which was found in the wall of nearby Netley Castle and probably came from Netley Abbey.

NETLEY

ST EDWARD'S CHURCH C1955 / N10004

NETLEY

VICTORIA ROAD c1955 / N10003

Pevsner described Netley as 'a Victorian period piece'; its streets of neat family villas and rows of renovated terraced cottages overlooking Southampton Water are certainly striking. Drive through the village and before long you reach the entrance to the Royal Victoria Country Park, formerly the site of the old Netley Hospital.

This imposing building is impressively situated on the shores of Southampton Water. The original castle, built by Henry VIII in 1542 as part of his many coastal defences, has all but disappeared, and was replaced by a large Victorian mansion during the 1880s. However, one surviving relic could be the Tudor archway in the main entrance, possibly part of the old fort.

NETLEY

THE CASTLE c1955 / N10085

Today, the chapel, with its distinctive green dome, is all that remains of the old Royal Victoria Military Hospital, opened in 1868 and demolished in 1966. The building was an incredible quarter of a mile long and cost more than £300,000 to construct. The sick, dying and injured were brought here from the war-torn corners of the British Empire; the 570-ft-long pier enabled casualties to be carried ashore from troop ships.

NETLEY

THE HOSPITAL 1908 / 60465

This must be one of the last photographs of the old military hospital at Netley before most of it disappeared from the shores of Southampton Water in a huge heap of rubble. It was Queen Victoria who originally argued the need for such a hospital; its objective was to care for the gravely-afflicted casualties of war. The building attracted criticism, and a mix-up with the plans resulted in the hospital being built the wrong way round, so that all the wards faced the sunless north.

NETLEY

THE ROYAL VICTORIA HOSPITAL c1955 / N10014

Famous as a yachting centre, Hamble has long thrived on its close proximity to the river of the same name, with its shipbuilding associations, yacht clubs and marinas. Originally a small fishing village renowned for oysters, crabs and lobsters, Hamble was later to become a sprawling community with the accent on leisure and the aircraft industry.

HAMBLE

THE QUAY c1955 / H148023

HAMBLE

THE VILLAGE c1955 / H148123

Despite the steady encroachment of urban and residential development along the shores of Southampton Water, we may be thankful that the quaint little village of Hamble remains intact. Its popularity with visitors ensures that its beauty is preserved and protected for future generations.

Pevsner likened Hamble to a West Country fishing village, and he was right to make the comparison. With its steep, winding streets and pretty cottages, there is a definite hint of Devon or Cornwall about it. Take a stroll through the village and you will be surprised at just how many pubs there are. The Victory Inn can be seen down the street, and round the corner, not visible in this picture, is The Bugle, Hamble's famous riverside inn, which probably dates from the 12th century.

HAMBLE

THE VILLAGE c1955 / H148035

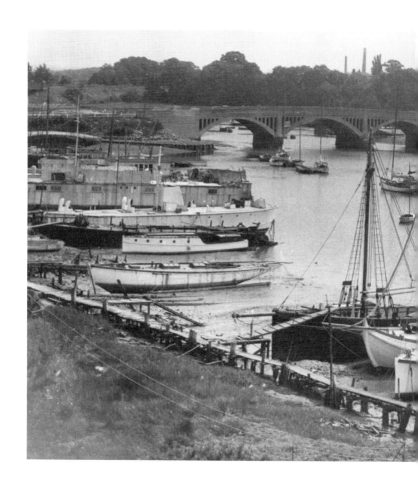

BURSLEDON

THE BRIDGE c1955 / B304008

Between the 14th and early 19th centuries, Bursledon was an important centre for naval shipbuilding, with the wooded slopes of the River Hamble providing much of the timber. HMS 'Elephant', Nelson's 74-gun flagship at the Battle of Copenhagen, was built here by George Parsons and launched at his yard in 1786.

BURSLEDON

THE RIVER c1960 / B304005

Until the beginning of the 19th century the only crossing of the Hamble was by ferry. The first structure was a toll bridge; today the river is spanned by various busy roads and a motorway—a far cry from the days centuries ago when this river and many others like it on the south coast were coveted by invaders.

BURSLEDON

HAMBLE RIVER c1955 / B304020

Bursledon village consists of two distinct halves—the new and the old.
The older part is more interesting and certainly more picturesque, with
its streets of quaint old buildings clinging to the banks of the Hamble.
Visitors to Bursledon often recall the little Gothic belfry at the entrance
to the Roman Catholic Chapel of Our Lady of the Rosary.

BURSLEDON

THE VILLAGE c1960 / B304003

OLD BURSLEDON

THE CHURCH c1965 / O112043

The church stands halfway up a hill overlooking the village rooftops and contains a large and impressive Norman font. The chancel arch is 13th-century, and the church contains several memorials to former shipbuilders, including Philemon Ewer, who died in 1750. Ewer built seven large ships of war for his majesty's service during the wars with France and Spain.

OLD BURSLEDON

THE VILLAGE c1965 / O112037

OLD BURSLEDON

THE POST OFFICE c1965 / O112033

CADNAM

THE SIR WALTER TYRRELL c1960 / C3020

This well-known inn is situated in a peaceful corner of the New Forest, close to Cadnam. Originally the pub was sited nearby and was known as the Stump, named after the one-legged landlady who ran it. It became the Sir Walter Tyrrell in 1929, but was destroyed by fire after the Second World War. It was later rebuilt. Sir Walter Tyrrell was a nobleman at the court of King William Rufus.

CADNAM

THE SIR WALTER TYRRELL c1960 / C3019

CADNAM

THE GREEN c1960 / C3024

Not very far from this spot lies the Rufus Stone, which marks the spot where King William Rufus, son of William the Conqueror, was accidentally killed by an arrow shot by Sir Walter Tyrrell while out hunting in nearby Canterton Glen in the summer of 1100. He had supposedly meant to kill a stag, but the arrow glanced and struck Rufus, the most hated of kings.

CADNAM

TWIN OAKS 1932 / 85061

A charming village scene that has scarcely changed at all in over 30 years. The old war-time nissen hut, at one time such a familiar sight in the British countryside, has gone, replaced by a car park and children's playground, and the thatched cottages have been renovated and re-thatched.

MARCHWOOD

THE VILLAGE c1965 / M315009

These redbrick cottages have defied the march of time and today look much as they did in the mid 1960s. Even the street lamp is still there. The cottages may look the same, but the surrounding landscape has changed virtually beyond recognition. Modern housing and industrial development crowd in from all directions, making it almost impossible to stand here and spot passing liners on Southampton Water.

MARCHWOOD

MAGAZINE LANE c1965 / M315004

ELING

THE QUAY c1955 / E252007

This photograph somehow conveys the feel of a picturesque West Country creek, with its thickly wooded shore and little boats stranded at low tide. The scene has changed little today. Nearby is Eling Tide Mill, the only surviving tide mill in the world still producing flour on a daily basis. Founded over 900 years ago, the site was restored and reopened in 1980 as a working mill and museum.

ELING

THE QUAY c1955 / E252006

Stand on the toll bridge by Eling Tide Mill, where this photograph was taken, and you will see that the tall chimney on the left has gone, as have many of the other industrial units seen in this photograph. Modern storage and container units have taken their place as the emphasis switches from industry to warehousing and unloaded cargo.

A short stroll from the toll bridge brings you to the little church of St Mary's. Above the altar hangs an impressive picture of the Last Supper. The chancel arch is a striking feature of the church, as is the 15th-century tower. Much has changed in this area of Hampshire, but little Eling, at the head of Southampton Water, is one tiny corner of the county that seems delightfully timeless.

ELING

ST MARY'S CHURCH c1955 / E252004

Totton, Eling's larger neighbour, once claimed the title of the 'largest village in Hampshire' —though it has expanded so much in recent years that by no stretch of the imagination could it still be described as a village. The old redundant 17th-century bridge over the Test now lies on the north side of the main road.

TOTTON

THE BY-PASS c1965 / T243010

Calshot has long been popular with local people and holidaymakers for the views it affords of Southampton Water. This stretch of the Hampshire coastline is the perfect spot to watch all the comings and goings on the water. This was the place to come to see the 'Queen Elizabeth' and the 'Queen Mary'—among other great liners from the great days of ocean-going travel.

CALSHOT

THE BEACH c1960 / C572001

By the Victorian drinking fountain at the entrance to Botley
station lies a memorial tablet which reads: 'this stone is erected to
perpetuate a most cruel murder committed on the body of Thomas
Webb, a poor inhabitant of Swanmore, on 11th February 1800
by John Diggins, a private soldier in the Talbot Fencibles, whose
remains are gibbeted on the adjoining common'.

BOTLEY

THE STATION c1960 / B544059

BOTLEY

THE MARKET HALL c1955 / B544027

This photograph shows the Dolphin Hotel on the right of the square, next to the mid-19th century Market Hall. In the days when Botley was an important staging post on the coach route, the village boasted as many as fourteen inns.

Situated at the western end of the main street, All Saints Church has dormer windows with carved barge-boards and a diamond-shaped clock with a gilded crown. The clock comes from the stables of the 19th-century farmer and journalist William Cobbett, who lived at Fairthorn Farm and described Botley as 'the most delightful village in the world'.

BOTLEY

ALL SAINTS CHURCH c1955 / B544001

BOTLEY

ALL SAINTS CHURCH 1960 / B544040

The clock on Botley's Market Hall is still a familiar landmark in the High Street. Just this side of it can be seen the premises of Botley Garages, now a sports shop and a hairdresser's. The swinging AA sign has gone, replaced by one for the sports unit. Small garages like this one were once a familiar sight in Britain's country towns and villages.

BOTLEY

HIGH STREET c1960 / B544035

Historian Arthur Mee described Botley as 'a delightful old town with quaint shops, handsome houses, and pretty inns'. William Cobbett was equally fulsome, maintaining that Botley had everything in it that he loved and nothing that he hated. However, he fell out with the local clergyman, declaring that he wanted to horsewhip him in the pulpit for talking such nonsense.

BOTLEY

SOUTHAMPTON ROAD c1955 / B544024

If you compare this photograph with the reality of the scene today, it would seem at first glance as if time has stood still here. However, look a little closer and you can pick out a few subtle changes. The white cottage on the right of the High Street is now the premises of an estate agent, and the ivy which covers the house on the left has gone. However, the portico and the telegraph pole remain. The white fencing on the right has disappeared and iron railings have been added. Typically, the Lloyds Bank branch has gone.

BOTLEY

HIGH STREET c1960 / B544045

BOTLEY

THE SQUARE c1955 / B544021

The bugler depicted in the pub sign has been replaced, and the old familiar shutters at the windows have gone. When this photograph was taken, this was a Strong's pub. However, the Romsey-based brewery, which was leased to Thomas Strong in 1858, was acquired by Whitbread in 1969 and brewing finally ceased in 1981.

BOTLEY

THE BUGLE INN c1960 / B544065

BOTLEY

On the extreme left is Botley Post Office, and next to it is a chemists; the former is now a dress shop, and the latter remains a pharmacy. The Dolphin, managed by Watneys when this photograph was taken, is now a Morland pub. Visit the Dolphin today and you can see that the clock face next to it is now an eye-catching black and gold.

BOTLEY

THE SQUARE c1955 / B544002

The splendid Market Hall has been home to two artefacts from the distant and recent past. One is a carved block of timber about three feet high, part of a Danish war galley found in the river during the 19th century; the other is a huge china jug adorned with ships and pictures, said to have been the punch jug used at the Farmers Club dinners in the days when Botley was a prosperous market town.

Here we see the sturdy porticoed front of Botley's famous Market Hall, built in 1848. The turret and clock above were erected by local parishioners to commemorate Queen Victoria's Diamond Jubilee in 1897. Opposite is the premises of W H Lewry, the High Street butcher, which remained in the family until 1999.

BOTLEY

THE SQUARE c1960 / B544044

Take a stroll down Church Lane and you can see that the scene on the right of this photograph has not changed at all. The little cottage on the left has been replaced by a redbrick house, and there is a modern bungalow just to the right of it. The partly timbered building with the large window and the gable end is still there, and is the premises of the local snooker club.

BOTLEY
CHURCH LANE C1955 / B544028

The right-hand side of the street has changed almost beyond recognition over the years. Maffey's has gone, and is now a private house with a portico. All the buildings beyond it have been demolished and replaced with modern development. The left-hand side of Winchester Road remains constant, with the pub and the timber-framed cottage still to be seen.

BOTLEY

WINCHESTER ROAD c1955 / B544019

The elegant Georgian house on the right of the road has been converted to offices. To the right of it is the entrance to Botley Mills, an 18th-century mill complex, which is mentioned in the Domesday Book. Just visible on the left of the picture is the stonework of the bridge which carries this road over the River Hamble.

BOTLEY

MILL HILL c1955 / B544005

EASTLEIGH

THE AIRPORT c1960 / E167030

Southampton Airport lies to the south of Eastleigh town centre; it was from here that the first Spitfire began her maiden flight in 1936. Many of the old buildings seen here have gone, replaced by an airport complex designed to meet the needs of the modern age.

Hampshire's only commercial airport was once at the centre of a major controversy. Both Southampton and Eastleigh laid claim to its title; the thorny problem was eventually and diplomatically settled by calling it Southampton (Eastleigh) Airport. Passengers and freight are conveyed by regular scheduled airlines to and from all corners of Britain, as well as the Channel Islands and Europe.

EASTLEIGH

THE AIRPORT c1960 / E167032

The buildings in this photograph look rather dated compared with today's modern airport complexes. The air traffic control centre is housed in a building which rather resembles an old war-time nissen hut; to the right of it is the quaintly-named emergency services rendezvous point.

EASTLEIGH

THE AIRPORT c1960 / E167025

Originally a village, Eastleigh expanded rapidly around Bishopstoke Junction after the London and South Western Railway Company's carriage works moved here in 1889-90, followed by the locomotive workshops in 1909. Many of the town buildings date from between 1890 and 1939, and many of its residents were employed by the railway.

EASTLEIGH

MARKET STREET c1955 / E167001

North Stoneham Church was rebuilt at the end of the 16th century in the Gothic style. One of the more unusual features of this church is the tombstone of 1491 which contains a group of Venetian sailors. These men may have been among the many trading fraternities using Southampton at that time.

EASTLEIGH

NORTH STONEHAM CHURCH c1960 / E167008

What the Army did for Aldershot, the London and South Western Railway Company did for Eastleigh, helping to transform a forgotten rural backwater into a bustling and thriving town. The image of the railway town remains, though many changes have taken place here in recent years. But Eastleigh is not just about railways. Many other forms of industry are based here, including Pirelli Cables and the Mr Kipling bakery.

EASTLEIGH

LEIGH ROAD c1960 / E167016

Ornate lamps and fashionable street furniture have been added to the High Street since this photograph was taken. The trees in the street have been pollarded, and the premises of John Cole and Delbridges have gone. A statue of the 'Railway Man' by sculptor Jill Tweed now stands on this corner, symbolising Eastleigh's link with the railway industry. The statue was unveiled in 1995.

EASTLEIGH

HIGH STREET c1960 / E167020

Modern Eastleigh is a grid pattern of late 19th-century and early 20th-century streets, with typical suburban fringes stretching out towards Southampton and Winchester. The geometric criss-crossing roads, the older buildings and the park with its bandstand give the town a separate identity from other towns in the region.

EASTLEIGH

HIGH STREET C1955 / E167019

EASTLEIGH

MARKET STREET c1960 / E167015

This photograph was taken about half-way along Market Street; it shows many shop premises, most of which have changed hands several times in the intervening years. Pricerite is now Peacocks, Lennards is the Abbey National Building Society and Dennis Cox acquired Dewhursts in the early 1990s. The tall, rather distinctive building on the left is now Burtons. The first floor was once a billiard room.

EASTLEIGH

MARKET STREET c1965 / E167044

EASTLEIGH

LEIGH ROAD c1960 / E167018

A fascinating photograph showing Leigh Road at its junction with Market Street. This corner of Eastleigh has changed significantly: the new buildings interposed with the older ones on the left-hand side of the street offer a rich mix of architectural styles. The street is now pedestrianised. The distant building with the steep roof is the Roman Catholic Church of Holy Cross.

EASTLEIGH

LEIGH ROAD c1960 / E167002

The old Town Hall is a dignified building of mellow brick with a clock beneath an elegant cupola. The building looks just the same now as it did in about 1960; nowadays, part of it is a dance and arts centre, together with a tourist information centre. Immediately beyond this fine building is The Park, a green lung at the centre of Eastleigh.

EASTLEIGH

THE TOWN HALL c1960 / E167022

EASTLEIGH

LEIGH ROAD c1960 / E167012

For so long Eastleigh has been synonymous with marshalling yards and the grime of the railway age. Over the years, the local planners have fought hard to improve the town's image, and in 1977 Eastleigh won a national competition for environmental improvement. Take a stroll through the town and you can see how the town has changed for the better in recent times.

Once a village, Chandlers Ford has now been swallowed up by the suburbs of nearby Southampton and Eastleigh. Chandler was the ancient miller who occupied the little mill in the valley; the ford was negotiated by passing stagecoaches.

CHANDLERS FORD
WINCHESTER ROAD c1965 / C490302

CHANDLERS FORD

THE PARADE c1960 / C490075

INDEX

PLEASE HELP US BRING FRITH'S PHOTOGRAPHS TO LIFE

Our authors do their best to recount the history of the places they write about. They give insights into how particular towns and villages developed, they describe the architecture of streets and buildings, and they discuss the lives of famous people who lived there. But however knowledgeable our authors are, the story they tell is necessarily incomplete.

Frith's photographs are so much more than plain historical documents. They are living proofs of the flow of human life down the generations. They show real people at real moments in history; and each of those people is the son or daughter of someone, the brother or sister, aunt or uncle, grandfather or grandmother of someone else. All of them lived, worked and played in the streets depicted in Frith's photographs.

We would be grateful if you would tell us about the many places shown in our photographs—the streets with their buildings, shops, businesses and industries. Describe your own memories of life in those streets: what it was like growing up there, who ran the local shop and what shopping was like years ago; if your workplace is shown tell us about your working day and what the building is used for now. With your help more and more Frith photographs can be brought to life, and vital memories preserved for posterity.

We will gradually add your comments and stories to the archive for the benefit of historians of the future. Wherever possible, we will try to include some of your comments in future editions of our books. Moreover, if you spot errors in dates, titles or other facts, please let us know, because our archive records are not always completely accurate—they rely on 150 years of human endeavour and hand-compiled records.

So please write, fax or email us with your stories and memories. Thank you!

CHOOSE ANY PHOTOGRAPH FROM THIS BOOK

for your FREE Mounted Print. Order further prints at half price

Fill in and cut out the voucher on the next page and return it with your remittance for £2.50 for postage, packing and handling to UK addresses (US $5.00 for USA and Canada). For all other overseas addresses include £5.00 post and handling. Choose any photograph included in this book. Make sure you quote its unique reference number eg. 42365 (it is mentioned after the photograph date. 1890 / 42365). Your SEPIA print will be approx 12" x 8" and mounted in a cream mount with a burgundy rule line (overall size 14" x 11").

Mounted Print
Overall size 14 x 11 inches

Order additional Mounted Prints at HALF PRICE - If you would like to order more Frith prints from this book, possibly as gifts for friends and family, you can buy them at half price (with no extra postage and handling costs) - only £7.49 each (UK orders), US $14.99 each (USA and Canada).

> *** IMPORTANT!**
> These special prices are only available if you order at the same time as you order your free mounted print. You must use the ORIGINAL VOUCHER on the facing page (no copies permitted). We can only despatch to one address.

Have your Mounted Prints framed (UK orders only) - For an extra £14.95 per print you can have your mounted print(s) framed in an elegant polished wood and gilt moulding, overall size 16" x 13" (no additional postage).

FRITH PRODUCTS AND SERVICES

All Frith photographs are available for you to buy as framed or mounted prints. From time to time, other illustrated items such as Address Books, Calendars, Table Mats are also available. Already, almost 50,000 Frith archive photographs can be viewed and purchased on the internet through the Frith website.

For more detailed information on Frith companies and products, visit

www.francisfrith.co.uk

For further information, trade, or author enquiries, contact:

The Francis Frith Collection, Frith's Barn, Teffont, Salisbury SP3 5QP
Tel: +44 (0) 1722 716 376 Fax: +44 (0) 1722 716 881 Email: sales@francisfrith.co.uk

Voucher

*for FREE
and Reduced Price
Frith Prints*

Do not photocopy this voucher. Only the original is valid, so please fill it in, cut it out and return it to us with your order.

	Picture ref no	Page number	Qty	Mounted @ £7.49 UK @$14.99 US	Framed + £14.95 (UK only)	US orders Total $	UK orders Total £
1			1	Free of charge*	£	$	£
2				£7.49 ($14.99)	£	$	£
3				£7.49 ($14.99)	£	$	£
4				£7.49 ($14.99)	£	$	£
5				£7.49 ($14.99)	£	$	£
6				£7.49 ($14.99)	£	$	£

Please allow 28 days for delivery

* Post & handling $5.00   £2.50

Total Order Cost US $ £

Title of this book . . . .

I enclose a cheque / postal order (UK) for £ . . . . $ . . . .
payable to 'Francis Frith Collection' (USA orders 'Frith USA Inc')

OR debit my Mastercard / Visa / Switch (UK) / Amex card / Discover (USA)
(credit cards only on non UK and US orders), card details below

Card Number

Issue No (Switch only)   Valid from (Amex/Switch)

Expires   Signature

Name Mr/Mrs/Ms . . . .

Address . . . .

. . . .

. . . .

Postcode/Zip. . . . . Country . . . .

Daytime Tel No . . . .   Valid to 31/12/06

PAYMENT CURRENCY: We only accept payment in £ Sterling or US $.
If you are ordering **from any other country, please pay by credit card**, and you will be charged in one of these currencies.